Be a
Wilderness
Detective

Peggy Kochanoff

NIMBUS
PUBLISHING

For my family (Stan, Tom, Jim, Avai, and Jaya), for their support.

Nimbus Publishing Limited
3731 Mackintosh St, Halifax, NS B3K 5A5
(902) 455-4286 nimbus.ca

Printed and bound in China

Author photo: Avai Kochanoff
Design: Jenn Embrce

Library and Archives Canada Cataloguing in Publication

Kochanoff, Peggy, 1943-
Be a wilderness detective : solving the mysteries of eastern Canadian fields, woods, and coastlines
     / Peggy Kochanoff.
Issued also in electronic format.
ISBN 978-1-77108-012-5

1. Natural history—Canada, Eastern—Miscellanea. I. Title.

QH106.K62 2013   508.713   C2012-907366-0

 Canada Council for the Arts   Conseil des arts du Canada   NOVA SCOTIA Communities, Culture and Heritage

Nimbus Publishing acknowledges the financial support for its publishing activities from the Government of Canada through the Canada Book Fund (CBF) and the Canada Council for the Arts, and from the Province of Nova Scotia through the Department of Communities, Culture and Heritage.

Table of Contents

Introduction and Acknowledgements

Playing outdoors is like a nature adventure. It is such fun climbing trees, chasing butterflies, calling to frogs, and collecting shells and feathers. By reading this book, you can try to solve some of the mysteries in nature, often found as close as your own doorstep. All you need is curiosity and patience. LOOK, LISTEN, SMELL, AND TOUCH!

I had a lot of help from Jim Wolford (a retired biology teacher at Acadia University, Nova Scotia) who checked all my nature facts and wording. Thanks so much.

Roy Bishop (doctorate in physics, Professor Emeritus at Acadia, past president of the Royal Astronomical Society of Canada) also helped me, making sure I got my tidal facts right. Thanks, Roy.

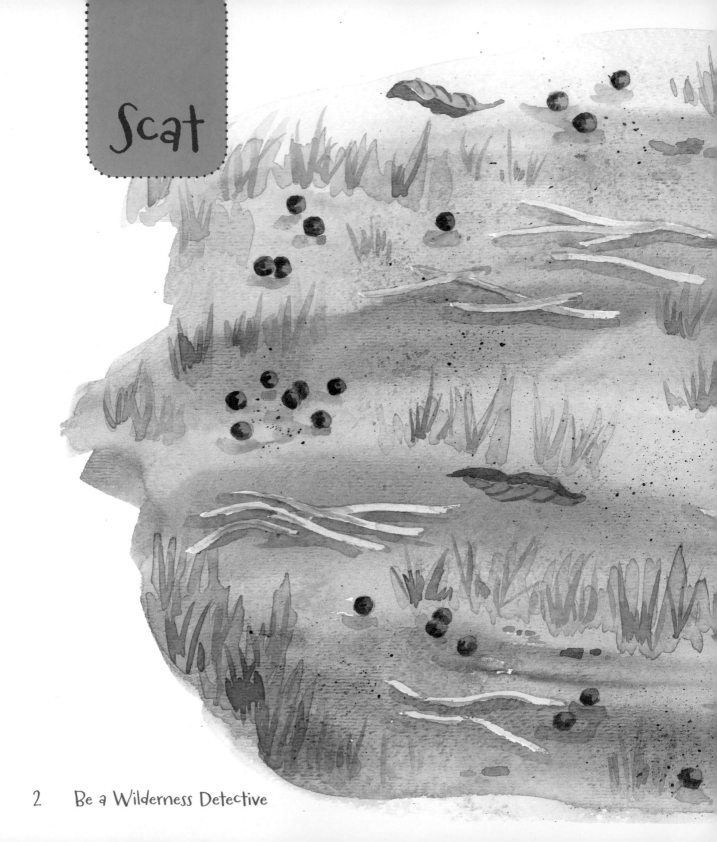

Scat

Hmmm...Who
pooped here?
Let's look closely
and find out.

ave you ever come upon wild animal poop (scientists call it "scat") during your walks? Don't be repulsed, because it is really interesting, but don't touch it with your hands because it can contain diseases or insects. Being able to identify poop means you can tell which animal passed your way—maybe just minutes before you.

Cottontail rabbit and hare scat is light brown, sawdust-like, and slightly flat. Hare scat is about 1.3 centimetres (0.5 inches) in diameter; cottontail rabbit scat is a little smaller.

Skunk scat is usually black and contains a lot of insect parts. It is medium-sized with blunt ends, and is 3.8 to 5 centimetres (1.5 to 2 inches) long, and about 1.3 centimetres (0.5 inches) in diameter.

Porcupine scat is very fibrous, since porcupines mainly eat bark. Their scat is made up of large numbers of oblong pellets, some slightly curved, some joined by thin strands, and it's often found in piles at the base of a tree or in a den site. It is 1.9 to 2.5 centimetres (0.8 to 1 inches) long, and 0.9 centimetres (0.4 inches) in diameter.

Fox and coyote scat has pointed ends, often with lots of hair, insect pieces, and bones (especially in fall and winter). Fox scat is 5 to 10 centimetres (2 to 4 inches) long, and 1.1 centimetres (0.4 inches) in diameter. Coyote scat is 5 to 12.7 centimetres (2 to 5 inches) long, and 1.9 centimetres (0.8 inches) in diameter.

Raccoon scat can be 7.6 to 15.2 centimetres (3 to 6 inches) long, though it usually breaks, and is 1.9 centimetres (0.8 inches) in diameter. It can be different colours, and you can see seeds or insect pieces within.

Deer scat consists of dark, cylindrical pellets with one pointed end and one flat or concave. There are often twenty to thirty pellets in one spot. The pellets are 1.9 to 2.5 centimetres (0.8 to 1 inch) long, and 0.9 centimetres (0.4 inches) in diameter.

🐾 Mystery solved! 🐾

Galls

Hmmm…Do you know what those weird growths on some plants are? Let's look closely and find out.

They are called galls, and they are amazing!

blueberry stem gall (from a wasp)

oak apple gall (from a wasp)

cherry black knot gall (from fungus)

willow petalled gall (from a midge)

gouty oak gall (from a wasp)

poplar purse gall (from an aphid)

pincushion rose gall (from a wasp)

These abnormal growths are caused by irritation to the plant tissues by chemicals from various parasites (midges and other flies, wasps, aphids, mites, nematodes, bacteria, and fungal spores).

An insect lays an egg in or on leaves, stems, buds, or twigs. When **larvae** hatch, their presence stimulates surrounding plant tissue to swell (much like when you have a splinter and your skin swells) and grow into strange, specific shapes. The gall provides protection for the larvae from weather and predators, and acts as a food supply. When the larvae become adults, they make little holes in the gall through which they can escape.

When a gall is produced by a fungus, new spores are released by moisture in the air, visiting insects, and even pruners, and they find new plant hosts.

Because galls form at specific sites on the plant, damage is limited and not all over the plant.

spruce pineapple gall (from an aphid)

goldenrod bunch gall (from a midge)

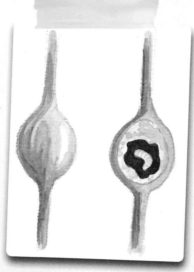

goldenrod elliptical gall (from a moth)

goldenrod ball gall (from a fly)

willow pinecone gall (from a gnat or midge)

maple leaf spindle gall (from a mite)

Mystery solved!

Tortoise Bugs

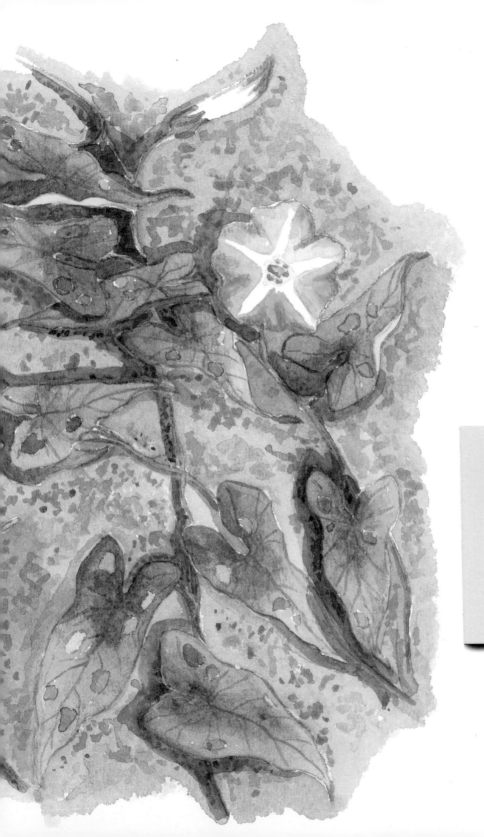

Hmmm…Who makes all the holes in the leaves of the wild morning glory (bindweed)? Let's look closely and find out.

It is the tortoise bug! You can usually find adults and larvae among the leaves of plants in the family that includes morning glory, sweet potatoes, and others with tubular flowers and often vines. Bindweed is usually the easiest to find.

The adults are a beautiful gold colour that glistens in the sun. The larvae are tan coloured, with some brown. They are constantly munching holes in the leaves. They have a hook that they hold over their back that collects bits of poop and skin they've shed. They wave this big, brown glob that forms at predators to scare them off. Try touching the glob gently with your fingers and watch it wave.

🌸 Mystery solved! 🌸

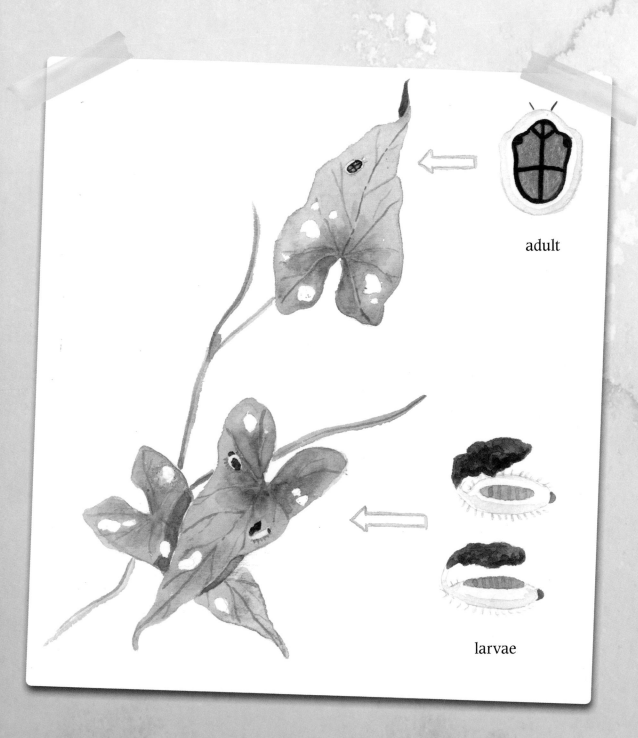

adult

larvae

Winter
Survival

Hmmm…How do the poor animals make it through the winter, when we are all bundled up?
Let's look closely and find out.

With the coming of the harsh weather of winter, the food supply of many animals decreases or stops. If they don't migrate, they have to adapt to these conditions. And there are many ways they adapt.

Some **mammals**, like deer, fox, beaver, and muskrat, go about life as usual but grow a thick winter coat that has insulating air pockets.

A few mammals, like ground squirrels, jumping mice, woodchucks, and many bats, hibernate.

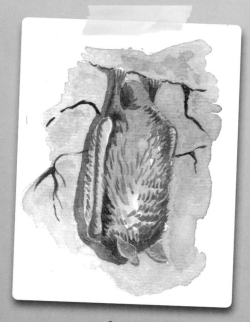

bat

woodchuck or groundhog

In true **hibernation**, body temperature decreases almost to that of the environment. Heartbeat and breathing slow dramatically. Since they are inactive, hibernating animals need little food and live off the energy they stored when they increased their food intake in the fall. They aren't sensitive to touch. Warming spring temperatures will finally arouse them.

raccoon

Other mammals go into a **dormant** state. Their temperature and metabolism slow somewhat, but they remain sensitive to touch and occasionally wake up to feed during winter thaws.

These mammals include bears, opossum, skunks, raccoons, badgers, and chipmunks.

bear

monarch butterfly

Insects are very resourceful over the winter. The adult monarch butterfly migrates to warmer climates.

Other insects make it through the winter as eggs. The adult lays the eggs and usually dies. Katydid eggs are laid along leaf edges, while praying mantis eggs survive in a hard case. Grasshopper and cricket eggs survive in soil.

katydid eggs

woollybear caterpillar

Some insects survive as larvae, like the woollybear caterpillar, which hides in leaf litter and may be active on warm winter days.

Some butterflies and moths survive as **pupae** attached to a branch, on the forest floor, or underground.

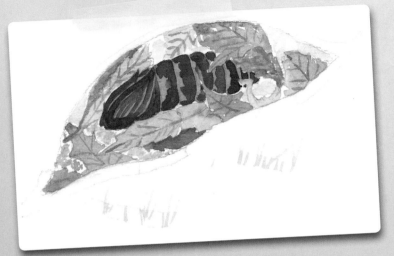

swallowtail butterfly pupa

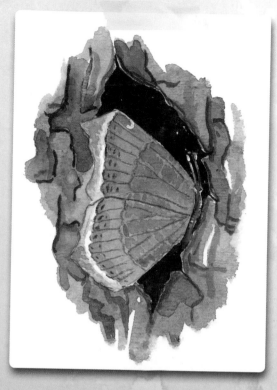

mourning cloak butterfly

Other insects survive as **nymphs** underwater, like mayflies, stoneflies, and dragonflies.

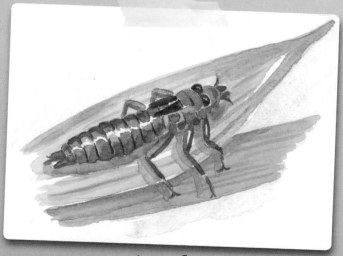

dragonfly

And some make it through the winter as adults. Mourning cloak butterflies hide in tree cracks. Queen bumblebees are snug in underground holes. Ladybird beetles pile together in large numbers in crevices. Ants huddle deep underground. All of these insects have antifreeze chemicals in their bodies.

Cold-blooded reptiles and amphibians also hibernate. Their body temperature drops to near freezing and their heartbeat becomes very slow. They can absorb oxygen from the water through their skin. Some develop a sugary antifreeze in their blood that helps protect their internal organs from freezing.

green frog

Toads burrow underground. Leopard frogs, green frogs, and some turtles burrow in mud under lakes and ponds.

garter snakes

Snakes eat a lot of food in the fall to gain body fat. Then in winter, large numbers curl together in underground burrows below the **frost line**.

Some fish, like yellow bullhead catfish, bury themselves at the bottom of lakes and ponds. Others, like bass, yellow perch, and pumpkinseed sunfish, hover almost motionless just off the bottom.

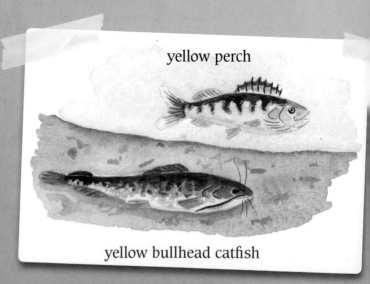

yellow perch

yellow bullhead catfish

Canada geese

Most birds migrate south to escape the cold northern climate.

chickadee

To keep warm, some birds fluff their feathers, creating air spaces that act as insulation. Others huddle together to share warmth.

cardinal

Those that stay feed on seeds, berries, hibernating insects, insect eggs, and dead matter. It's fun watching birds at a feeder!

🌸 Mystery solved! 🌸

Tree Rings

Hmmm...What are the rings on tree stumps and how did they get there? Let's look closely and find out.

Find a tree stump and carefully follow from the outside in.
The bark is on the outer edge and protects the tree against insects, excess water, extreme heat and cold, and fire.

Next are **phloem** cells. These tubes transport sugar produced during **photosynthesis** in the leaves to branches, trunk, and roots.

The **cambium** layer is only a few cells thick and can only be seen under a microscope. This layer is very important because on the outside it produces phloem cells and on the inside it produces **xylem** cells.

Xylem cells form tubes that bring water and nutrients from roots

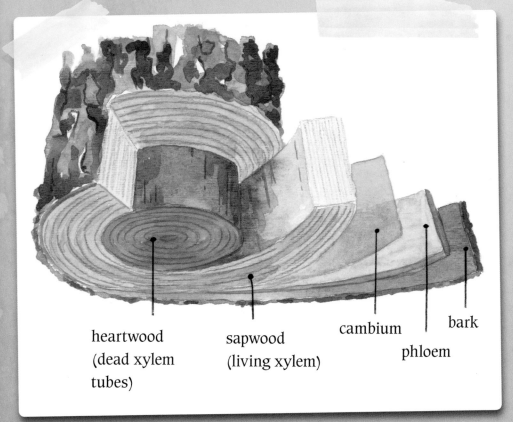

heartwood
(dead xylem
tubes)

sapwood
(living xylem)

cambium

phloem

bark

to leaves and other parts of the tree. In late winter and early spring, xylem transports sugar (changed from starch stored in the roots) to all parts of the tree. (To learn more about this sugar in maple trees, see page 32.)

Xylem cells form the tree rings you see. In spring, when growing conditions are best and wettest, xylem cells are large, thin-walled, and light-coloured. In the drier summer, cells are smaller, thick-walled, and dark-edged. These light and dark cells together form a ring. Fast, healthy growth produces wide rings. Slow growth (due to harsh conditions) produces narrow rings.

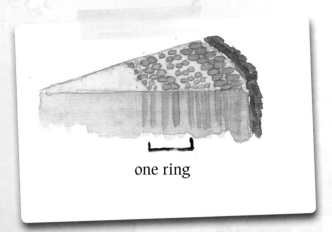

one ring

insect damage

wide rings (healthy, fast growth)

off-centre growth (maybe too shady on one side)

fire damage

narrow rings (slow growth)

read a cross-section
(thirteen rings means thirteen years)

🌸 Mystery solved! 🌸

Lichens

Hmmm...There is some weird stuff growing on trees and rocks. What could it be? Let's look closely and find out.

Lichens   29

That weird stuff is lichens. Lichens are actually two organisms together, an alga and a fungus. They live and work together in a partnership called **symbiosis**. The alga (which is microscopic) is a simple plant that makes food by photosynthesis. The fungus provides a place for the alga to grow, collects water like a sponge, collects minerals, and protects it from too much sun and wind. Lichens are very tough and survive from the Arctic to the Antarctic, under snow, in hot deserts, on rocks and trees, and in temperatures from extremely hot to brutally cold. Although they can live on wind-borne water and nutrients, most cannot survive in polluted air.

old man's beard

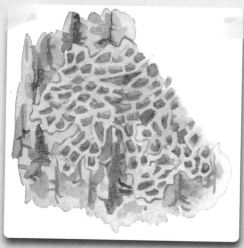

leafy lichen

crusty lichen

reindeer lichen

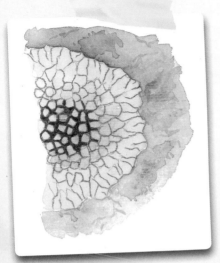

crusty lichen

British soldiers

leafy lichen

pixie cups

One of the most important things about lichens is that they are pioneers; they actually create soil. They are the first life forms to grow on bare rock surfaces. Because of the acid they secrete and their shrinking movements when they dry out, they cause small pieces of rock to slowly crumble away to form soil. It takes a long time, as most lichens only grow 1.3 centimetres (0.5 inches) a year, but after many years enough soil accumulates for other plants to grow.

There are fifteen thousand different kinds of lichens, in all shapes, sizes, and colours. Some are crusty, others are leaf-like, and others are unusual shapes with stalks.

❀ Mystery solved! ❀

Maple Sap

Hmmm...How do we get maple syrup, and docs it hurt the tree? Let's look closely and find out.

The sweet sap from which syrup is made is common to all maple trees (even some birch and walnut), but sugar maples have the highest yield and sweetest sap. While leaves are on the tree, sugar is made in the leaves, by photosynthesis. Phloem tubes transport this sugary sap from the leaves to branches, trunk, and roots. A lot of unused sugar is stored as starch in the roots at the end of the season. In late winter and early spring, starch is changed back into sugar, which is water-soluble, and moves in the sap from the roots through xylem tubes. In the regular growing season xylem brings water and nutrients from roots to the leaves and other parts of the tree. Sugar content in the sap reaches its highest concentration in late winter and early spring. The tree needs this food to start growing its buds, leaves, and branches.

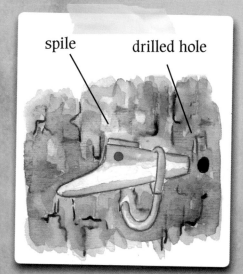

spile   drilled hole

People wanting to make maple syrup drill small holes with an 11-millimetre (0.4-inch) drill bit about 5 to 7.5 centimetres (2 to 3 inches) deep, pointing slightly upward (for drainage) into the tree. A **spile** is tapped in at once. Trees should be tapped on all sides, 0.6 to 1.5 metres (2 to 5 feet) up and 15 centimetres (6 inches) from the nearest tapping scar. When a pail is hung, it is covered to keep out debris. Modern syrup producers often use plastic tubing instead of pails to deliver sap to a central building. This saves a lot of labour.

inserted spile with pail hanging

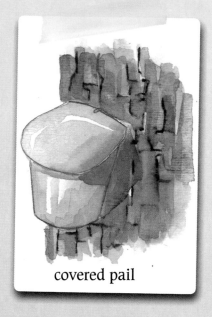

covered pail

Cross-section showing tap holes
that have healed in the xylem

Tapping doesn't hurt the tree, because tappers only take about 10 percent of the sugar produced annually, and they do not tap trees less than twenty-five centimetres (ten inches) in diameter.

Tap holes do affect the adjacent wood. Sapwood (the living xylem tubes) dries out and dies in a strip equal to the depth of the hole and a little wider than the adjacent wood. Dead wood extends 2.5 to 5 centimetres (1 to 2 inches) above and below the hole. Dead areas can't be tapped until new wood forms. The tree heals in one to two years.

However it's collected, sap is boiled within twenty-four hours of its collection. Since it takes 151 litres (40 gallons) of sap to produce 3.7 litres (1 gallon) of syrup, a lot of water needs to boil off. If you have a sugar maple (check in a guide, since so many maple trees look similar), collect some sap and taste it for sweetness, then boil it for a while and taste it when it is more concentrated. Yum!

🌼 Mystery solved! 🌼

Fireflies

Hmmm...How can fireflies give off light and not become hot like an electric light bulb? Let's look closely and find out.

A firefly, which is really a kind of beetle, is more than 92 percent efficient in converting energy into light. An ordinary incandescent light bulb is only 10 percent efficient, which means 90 percent of the energy is given off as heat. Fireflies produce what is called "cold light." An organic substance called luciferin and an **enzyme** called luciferase react together with oxygen to produce cold light in fireflies as well as some other insects, sea creatures, and worms. Cold light can be yellow, light green, or pale red. Most fireflies produce yellow-green light but some species can produce the other colours too.

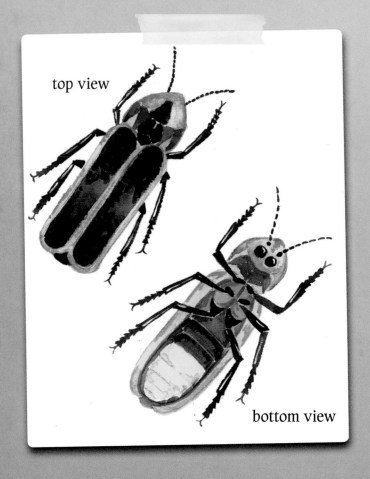

top view

bottom view

On warm summer nights where the grass isn't cut too short, look for flashes of light. This flashing is a mating signal given off by the male firefly, who is flying in the air, to the female, who is on the ground. Once she recognizes the flash of her own species, she gives an answering flash. Firefly flashes differ in several ways: the time of night they occur, the length of the flash, the time between flashes, the number of flashes, and the colour of flashes. It is amazing that fireflies can find each other at night using these beautiful flashing lights.

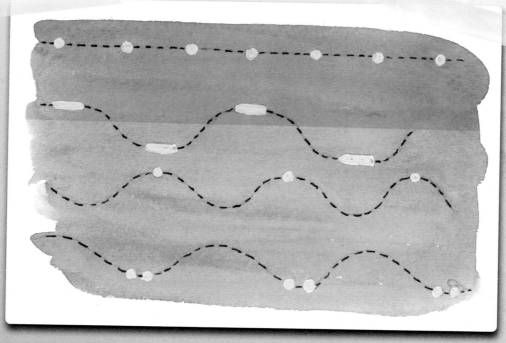

different flash patterns

🐞 Mystery solved! 🐞

Tides

Hmmm...What causes
the tides?
Let's look closely and
find out.

low tide

high tide

Be a Wilderness Detective

The moon's gravity pulls strongest on the near side of the planet Earth, causing a bulge in the ocean waters there. Similarly, Earth itself feels a stronger pull from the moon than does the ocean water on its far side, pulling Earth away from the waters there, resulting in another tidal bulge.

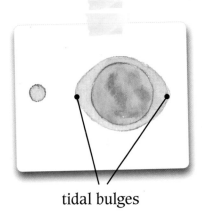

tidal bulges

Like the moon, the sun's pull also causes two bulges in the ocean waters, but because the sun is so far away, its bulges are less than half as big as those of the moon. During a new moon (shown) or a full moon (on the side of Earth opposite the sun), the sun's and moon's tidal bulges are aligned, making extra high **"spring" tides** (the name has no relation to the season).

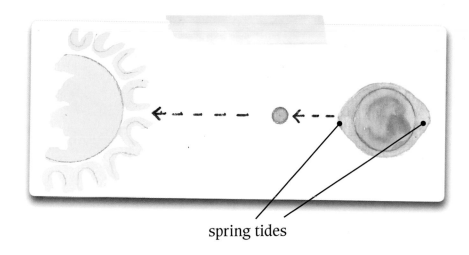

spring tides

When the sun and moon are at right angles (90°) to each other (during a quarter moon), the sun's smaller tidal effect reduces that of the moon, resulting in lower **"neap" tides**.

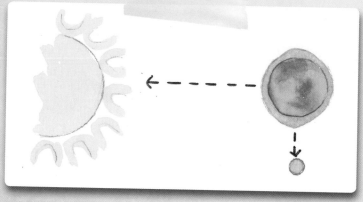

neap tides

In most places there are two high and two low tides each day. The bulges align with the moon, because Earth turns once every twenty-four hours while the moon orbits the earth every twenty-seven days. This causes the tides to operate on the moon's schedule, which is fifty minutes later every day. Since there are two sets of tides each day, the high tides will be about twelve hours and twenty-five minutes apart from each other, as will the low tides.

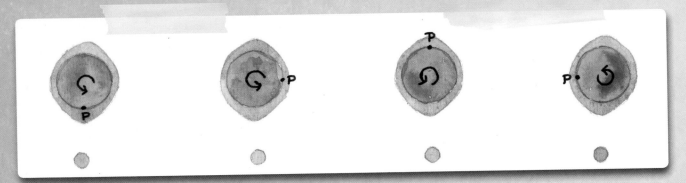

P (shown rotating on four Earth positions)

As Earth rotates each day, a person at point P experiences two high and two low tides.

Once liquid in a basin is set in motion, it has a typical cycle of fluctuating back and forth. The time period for water to slosh from side to side in the Bay of Fundy and the Gulf of Maine (which are connected) is nearly equal to the twelve hours and twenty-five minutes of the Atlantic Ocean.

Imagine the water in the Bay of Fundy as a person on a swing going back and forth. Tides from the Atlantic Ocean are like a person giving an extra push to the swinger moving forward. This increases the tide flowing toward the head of the Bay of Fundy. The length and depth of a body of water also influences the height of tides. Fundy tides are the highest in the world!

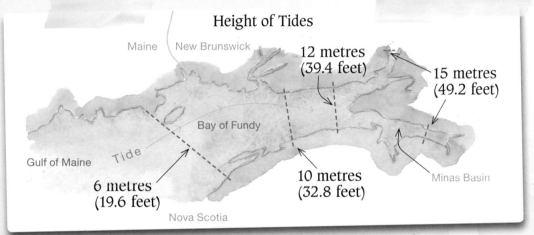

Height of Tides

Maine — New Brunswick

12 metres (39.4 feet)

15 metres (49.2 feet)

Bay of Fundy

Gulf of Maine — Tide

6 metres (19.6 feet)

10 metres (32.8 feet)

Minas Basin

Nova Scotia

The **tidal bore** is very special. It is a wave formed by the edge of the incoming tide that travels against the natural current of a bay or river. It's great fun to raft on this wave, especially during the highest tides.

tidal bore

❧ Mystery solved! ❧

Sandpipers

Hmmm…How can so many birds find enough food on the mud flats? Let's look closely and find out.

When the tide goes out in the Bay of Fundy, vast areas of red-brown mud are exposed. In this mud live tiny, 9.5-millimetre (0.4-inch) long mud shrimp, feeding on **diatoms** and organic particles. They also come out of their U-shaped burrows to look for mates. At low tide, without the protection of water, the shrimp are vulnerable to hungry birds. In the Bay of Fundy, with ideal conditions, 1 square metre (10.8 square feet) of mud averages ten thousand to twenty thousand shrimp. Sometimes there can be as many as sixty thousand! Because these shrimp are high in fat, birds can double their weight in ten to twenty days. Nowhere else can the birds find such huge quantities of high-energy food to prepare them to fly non-stop from the Maritimes to their wintering grounds in South America.

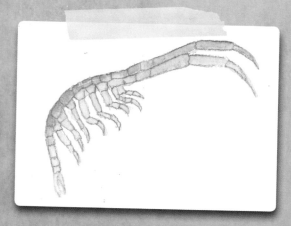

Corophium volutator (mud shrimp)

U-shaped burrows

Every summer, the upper Bay of Fundy hosts massive flocks of shorebirds coming from northern Canada on their migration south. They include black-bellied plovers, semipalmated plovers, least sandpipers, white-rumped sandpipers, two kinds of yellowlegs, and other species. The most abundant bird found there is the semipalmated sandpiper—95 percent of its total world population is found on these mudflats! Over two million semipalmated sandpipers move through the Bay of Fundy every year. When the tide comes in and covers the flats, birds roost along the shore in huge numbers. The slightest disturbance causing them to fly away from the shore depletes their precious reserve of stored energy, which they'll need to migrate to South America.

Mud flats of the Bay of Fundy are a very important habitat for worms, shrimp, crabs, snails, and more. If something should cause the mud shrimp population to decline, the effect on the shorebirds could be devastating!

semipalmated sandpiper

🌸 Mystery solved! 🌸

Wilderness Activities

Galls. Look around for a goldenrod gall. It is easiest to see in winter when vegetation dies back. If there is a tiny hole in the gall, the insect inside has already left. Find a gall without a hole and have an adult cut it open. You should find a tiny white larva inside. When you are done observing, replace the larva and the gall.

Tortoise bugs. Try to find some wild morning glory (bindweed) with holes in the leaves. Look closely to find the small larva. Wiggle your finger and you should see the larva wave its "hook" back at you.

Winter survival. In winter, look closely at tree bark, branches, and leaf debris and try to find hidden overwintering insects, pupa, or eggs.

Tree rings. Find a tree stump (check with the owner if it isn't on your property) and count the rings to find the tree's age. Also look for narrow rings (harsh conditions), wide rings (good conditions), and insect or fire damage.

Lichens. See how many different lichens (shapes, colours) you can find by looking on tree trunks, rocks, gravestones, and old pieces of metal. They are everywhere! You can use a guide book or the internet to help you identify them by name.

Maple syrup. If you are near a sugar maple (if it isn't yours, get permission), buy a spile at a hardware store and have an adult drill a hole and insert it. Collect some sap in late February or early March (depending on the weather—maple sap starts to move inside the tree when nights are below freezing but days are above) and taste it for sweetness. Boil it down for a while (you will get a lot of steam). Remember, it takes an awful lot of sap to make any syrup! Don't worry about being too precise, just boil the sap until it is thicker. Enjoy the sweet taste on some pancakes. Yum!

Fireflies. On a warm summer night, take a flashlight and try to copy the flashes you see. Try to collect a few fireflies in a jar to see up close. Release them when you are done.

Tides. If you live near the ocean, go to a beach at high tide. Mark the highest point with rocks or sticks and record the time. The next day, go to the beach at the same time and see where the tide reaches.

Glossary

cambium. The growing layer of cells beneath tree bark.

cold-blooded. A cold-blooded creature doesn't produce its own body heat and is sensitive to surrounding temperatures.

diatoms. Single-celled algae in fresh or marine water.

dormant. A sleep-like state from which an animal will occasionally wake to feed and eliminate wastes.

enzyme. An organic substance that will increase the rate of a chemical reaction.

frost line. The point in the ground below which frost doesn't penetrate.

hibernation. A physical state of an animal in which all body functions slow down to conserve energy. The animal isn't easily awakened.

larva. Immature stage of an animal.

mammal. An animal that is warm-blooded, breathes air, and has hair and a backbone. The female produces milk for the infant.

metamorphosis. Development from an egg to an adult.

neap tides. Lowest tides of the lunar month, when the sun and moon are at right (90°) angles.

nymph. Young of an insect with gradual **metamorphosis**.

phloem. Tubes located just under the bark that carry sugar (produced by photosynthesis) in the leaves to all parts of the tree via the sap.

photosynthesis. The process by which a plant or tree forms sugars from carbon dioxide, water, and sunlight using the chlorophyll in its leaves, and releases oxygen as a waste product.

pupa. A stage of development between larva and adult in complete metamorphosis

spile. A spout driven into a sugar maple to let sap drip into a bucket.

spring tides. Exceptionally high and low tides that occur when the Moon and Sun are aligned.

symbiosis. Two organisms living together in a mutally beneficial relationship (like lichens).

tidal bore. Wave formed by the edge of the incoming tide travelling against the natural current.

xylem. Tubes that carry water and minerals from roots to leaves and other parts. In late winter and early spring, the tubes carry sugar from the roots to the rest of the tree. Living tubes are called sapwood. Older, inner-most, dead tubes are called heartwood.

Suggested Resources

Nature Books for Kids

Boring, Mel and Diane Burns. *Fun With Nature*. New York: Northword Books, 1998.

Burnie, David and Richard Walker. *Nature Ranger*. New York: DK Children, 2006.

Conant, Roger and Robert Stebbins. *Guide to Reptiles and Amphibians*. Boston: Houghton Mifflin, 1999.

Fredericks, Anthony. *Under One Rock: Bugs, Slugs and Other Ughs*. Nevada City, CA: Dawn Publications, 2001.

Landstrom, Lee Ann and Karen Shragg. *Nature's Yukky: Gross Stuff That Helps Nature Work*. Missoula, MT: Mountain Press, 2003.

Leahy, Christopher. *Peterson First Guide to Insects of North America*. Boston: Houghton Mifflin, 1998.

Milord, Susan. *The Kid's Nature Book: 365 Indoor/Outdoor Activities and Experiences*. Charlotte, VT: Williamson Publishing, 1996.

lmstead, Adrienne. *My Nature Journal: A Personal Nature Guide for Young People*. Lafayette, CA: Pajaro, 1999.

Selsam, Millicent. *Where Do They Go? Insects in Winter*. New York: Four Winds Press, 2001.

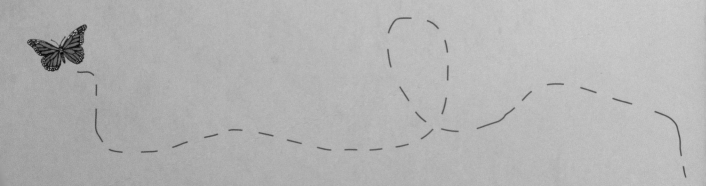